For:

SEASON *of* LIGHT

Treasured Traditions of Christmas

By John P. Beilenson

Designed by Pink, Inc.

PETER PAUPER PRESS, INC.
WHITE PLAINS, NEW YORK

For Wanda and Carly, the light of my Christmases

*Thanks to Irene Scatliff for her help in identifying
Scandinavian Christmas traditions, and to Cary
Limberakis for assistance on Greek traditions*

Title page art copyright © 1996 Judith Ann Griffith.
Art page 42 copyright © 1996 James Henterly.
Title page and page 42 art licensed by InterArt
Licensing, Bloomington, IN.

Contents

*C*hristmas throughout the world is the season of light, a time when Christians of many countries, each through their own traditions, celebrate the birth of the Savior.

Central to Christmas is the star that rose above Bethlehem and announced to the world that Jesus, "the Light of the World," had been born. The great star, a beacon of peace, led the Three Wise Men to the manger where the baby Jesus lay. The star is a powerful reminder that winter's darkness, and by extension the darkness of the human heart, will give way to the light. Today, Christians throughout the world celebrate this miracle—the light that Christ's birth shone on the world—in endlessly diverse and lovely ways.

One of the most charming Christmas traditions—placing lights in a window—comes from Ireland. There, each family hoped that a priest would come to its home to celebrate Christ's birth during Holy Night. Families left their doors unlocked and placed lit candles in the window to guide priests through the dark to their warmly lit homes. Today, illumination in windows, whether by candles or lamps, is an elegant holiday accent, inviting the spirit of Christmas to grace our homes.

In the American Southwest, candles play a delightful role at Christmas. From Los Angeles to Louisiana, thousands of *luminarias*—paper bags containing sand-secured lighted candles—enliven narrow streets and driveways or sit perched on garden walls and flat rooftops. This tradition originated in Spain and later found its way to Mexico. While today the *luminarias* serve as beautiful holiday decorations, they were traditionally used, like the Irish window lights, as guides for priests as they made their way on evening visits during the Christmas season.

In Russian communities, Christmas Eve often involves the procession known as *Krestny Khod* ("walking with the Cross"). In a tradition dating back more than 1,000 years, Russian Orthodox priests lead their congregants, holding candles, or bearing religious flags and icons, around their church. When the circumambulation is complete, the worshipers re-enter the chapel and sing hymns or carols before heading home for a late Christmas Eve dinner.

In a less formal "starlit" procession, Romanian boys and girls travel from house to house carrying a large wooden star or *steaua* mounted on a broomstick or pole. The star, coated with shiny paper, decorated with bells and colored ribbon, and lit by a candle, often frames a picture of the Holy Family at its center.

Swedish Christmas invariably includes girls dressed as Santa Lucia (the patron saint of seafarers) and her handmaidens. Santa Lucia is clothed in a simple white nightgown with a red sash around her waist, and wears on her head a wreath lit with beeswax candles. Each December 13 (the Feast Day of Santa Lucia), Santa Lucia and her similarly clad handmaidens serenade their friends and others with traditional songs at public gatherings. At home, daughters dressed as Santa Lucia serve their mothers a delicious breakfast in bed, including strong coffee, saffron buns, and delicious spice cookies.

In some places, the "light" of Christmas can be more explosive. In Spain and Latin America, fireworks are set off to mark the end of the holiday, which occurs on January 6, the Feast of the Epiphany.

A Miraculous Birth

~ ~

ADAPTED FROM THE 1875 STORY
BY STEVEN T. ANDERSON

*T*am a woman who loves the spirit of Christmas. So, along with my loving husband and three lively children, I make sure that each Christmas holiday is special. We make our own ornaments. Going to the tree farm to cut down exactly the right tree is a big event. In our house, Santa has not only a glass of milk waiting for him on Christmas Eve, but some delicious home-made cookies as well. In fact, it wasn't always this way. My love affair with Christmas started on a cold, blustery Christmas Eve, now some 30 years ago.

I remember it as if it were yesterday. The wind was blowing, and I was tired of all our traditional family Christmas fuss. I was, sad to say, something of a cynic, a grinch, a scrooge, if you will. I spent the weeks leading up to the holiday announcing to my family how "fake" and commercial Christmas had become. I was furious that my brothers and sisters and, it seemed, the whole world placed so much emphasis on presents and so little emphasis on the religious part of the holiday. I was both self-righteous and a cynic. I was 14!

On Christmas Eve everyone was busy around the tree or in the kitchen. So, hearing the wind blowing, I decided to put on my coat and get a little air. We lived in a relatively new suburb quite close to a state park. Leaving the neatly lit streets around my house, I stumbled across an uneven field and up a short, well-trod path that climbed Henderson's Knoll. There was just enough moon to help me

make my way, and soon I was at the top. It was one of my favorite places to come and think or to skip out with a couple of friends and maybe, if truth be told, smoke a cigarette. On Christmas Eve, though, I was all alone and looked up at the sky, which was filled with the light of stars.

I sat there for a while thinking about my friends and boys and school, and then I thought, "I'm just as bad as my family; I should be thinking about Mary and Joseph and the Christ child." And when the wind blew, it was not too hard to imagine the Holy Family, cold and frightened, looking for a place to rest. Looking back at the sky, I was drawn to one particularly bright star. Warming to the holiday spirit, I decided that it was indeed in the East, and that I would follow it, in search of the Prince of Peace himself.

I got off my perch, made my way down the knoll, and headed in the direction of the star. The town's street lamps obscured some of the lights above, but that star kept shining, kept drawing me on. Soon I was in familiar territory, tracing the path I took each Tuesday and Thursday afternoon to ride at the Double R Stables. Things looked pretty quiet, but I hopped the gate and made my way back to the stables. No one was around, but I figured I would just check in on Joe Bob, a solid, respectable gelding, and I unhitched the latch and went in.

Joe Bob was fine, munching quietly on his Christmas ration of oats, but I noticed that something was amiss. In the next stall, Mary Jane, a fine roan mare with an even temperament, was lying on the floor. She was wide-eyed and breathing heavily. I went to open the gate on her stall, but that only provoked Mary Jane to more thrashing. I held my ground. I may have watched her for one minute or one hour, I can't recall. What I remember to this day was her breathing, and the slow, steady progress— head, then body, then legs—of a shiny newborn colt.

A miracle, I thought to myself. For all my cynicism, God had chosen to show me on Christmas the miracle of creation, a sign of His boundless love. I returned to my home, flushed with excitement and told my family what I had witnessed. From their rapt and smiling faces, I began to form an appreciation of the countless, everyday miracles required first to create and then to bond a family—even mine. So whenever I hear someone—and my oldest daughter will be 14 in March—complain about the commercialism of Christmas, the fakery, I have to smile. I think back to that cold, December evening, when a bright and shining star led me to an understanding of the power and the glory that is Christmas.

*T*ucked into the coldest part of the Northern Hemisphere's year, Christmas celebrates not only light, but heat—that is, fire. The Christmas Yule log dates back to ancient Persia. There, the *yole* was a round wheel cut from the trunk of an old tree. The wheel was meant to represent the entire year, and with each season one-quarter of the circle was burned. As winter arrived, it was time to burn the last section of the *yole*. Our Yule traditions derive from this Eastern practice, although they arrived in America influenced by Scandinavian and particularly British customs.

Throughout Scandinavia, Yuletide or *jul* (from the older *hjul*, or wheel) refers to the sun "turning" toward springtime and the new year. Historically, it was an auspicious time, when one's fortunes for the coming year were determined. In each home, the Yule log (really an entire tree) burned slowly—from the roots to the tips—for the whole of the season, protecting the household from evil spirits.

In medieval England lords felled a large tree during Yuletide. It was often an ash tree, as legend had it that Mary saw the baby Jesus for the first time by the light of an ash wood fire. They then cut and marked a section of the trunk, and hid it. During Christmas, the people who lived on the manor went in search of the massive log. When the people found the "Yule" log, they dragged it into the main hall of the manor, which was thrown open for all to enjoy. Hauled onto the fire, the log caught flame, a signal for the entire community to begin its Christmas festivities.

While the feudal associations of this tradition did not emigrate to the colonies, the Yule log did. Today, for many, of English ancestry or not, Christmas is not complete without a warm fire in the fireplace, a thick log burning slowly throughout the day.

This is not to say that all Christmas blazes burn indoors. In the Desert Southwest, pitch bonfires or *farolitos*, a Latin American tradition imported from Spain, are traditionally lit on each of the nine nights preceding Christmas. These welcoming blazes symbolize the nine days Mary and Joseph needed to travel, often looking for warmth and shelter, from Nazareth to Bethlehem to be counted in the Roman census.

Greek traditions combine a little Yule and a little *farolito*. Rural folk light fires to prevent the *kalikántzari*, mischievous goblins particularly active at Christmas, from scampering down the chimney. Thus a Christ log or *skarkántzalos*, burns from Christmas to the Epiphany. In some villages, large bonfires are built to scare off the *skarkántzalos*. The most skittish townsfolk even carry a candle with them at night for protection.

*I*n English, the word "Christmas" comes from "Christ-mass" referring to the church festival surrounding the birth of the Savior. The Dutch have a similar word, *Kerst-misse.* In Spain *(El Natal)* and Italy *(Il Natale)*, these words celebrate "the birth," the miracle of Christ's arrival. Linguistically, these words bear resemblance to the ancient Roman feast day, *Dies Solis Invicti Nati*, the Birth of the Unconquered Sun. The French *Noël* also means "birthday," though today *Noëls* are also French Christmas Carols.

In Germany, *Weihnachten* means "Watch night," as Christmas Eve there has long been associated with miracles. It has been reported that on Christmas Eve trees have burst into blossom out of season, and mountains have fissured to reveal lodes of gems. Of course, most miraculous of all was that the Virgin Mary gave birth to the Christ-child on the very first Christmas. So it is indeed, for all of us, a night to keep close watch.

*F*or children especially, Christmas is indeed the happiest day of the year.

While the celebration of Christ's Mass dates back to the early days of the Church, gift-giving on Christmas Day is considerably more recent. In England, the practice began during the reign of Queen Victoria and was probably then imported to the United States. Previously, gifts were exchanged on New Year's Day or Twelfth Night (January 5) or even on the Feast of the Epiphany. England has also developed a second gift day around Christmas. On Boxing Day (December 26), the alms boxes at each church are opened and the contents distributed to the poor. Traditionally, private and public servants, employed on Christmas, are given the 26th off, and take the opportunity to open their tip boxes that day. Today, both Christmas Day and Boxing Day are national holidays in Great Britain.

In Germany and Scandinavia, Christmas Eve is generally reserved for gifts. In Greece, where the holidays of Christmas, New Year's Day, and Epiphany are combined into a period called the *Dodecameron* (literally, "twelve days"), gift-giving is nevertheless reserved for Christmas Eve day. Greek children proceed from house to house singing *kálanda* (carols) and carrying small ships of cardboard, wood, or tin in honor of St. Basil, who came to Greece by sea to bring presents to children. At each home, the ships are filled with candy and other treats.

In Italy, Spain, and parts of Latin America, gifts are given on the Feast of the Epiphany, January 6. In the Netherlands and Russia, presents are given on the Feast Day of St. Nicholas, December 6. In Japan, although New Year's Day is the most important day in the Japanese calendar, Japanese Christians nonetheless continue to exchange gifts on Christmas Day.

*W*hether you call him *Sankt Nikolaus* in German, *Sinterklaas* in Dutch, Santa Claus, or old St. Nick, Saint Nicholas, the patron saint of young people, has always been associated with Christmas, and, of course, with gifts. And while today his ruddy likeness, red suit, reindeer, and propensity for sliding his thick frame down the chimney are all familiar, Nicholas of Tyra was in fact a 3rd-century religious man in Asia Minor whose generosity caused him to be elevated to sainthood.

Nicholas was born in the Turkish port city of Patara and orphaned early in his life, but inherited a great deal of wealth. Nevertheless, he dedicated his life to God. As a young man, he moved to Tyra, the province's chief city. Arriving at church as usual one morning, Nicholas was surprised to find an elderly

clergyman in the doorway. The man, charged
with finding Tyra's next bishop, had received a
dream the night before. The first person to enter
the church, it prophesied, would be the next
bishop. At first Nicholas attempted to refuse this
surprising honor. He was prevailed upon, however,
and indeed took up the high position.

Historians tell us that Nicholas traveled to
Jerusalem early in his career. He was so taken
by the place connected so intimately with Christ's
life that he resigned his office and stayed in the
Holy Land. Nicholas returned to Asia Minor in
303 A.D. to defend Christians who were being
persecuted by the Roman Emperor Diocletian,
and was imprisoned for a time until Diocletian's
successor, Constantine, proclaimed a tolerance
for all religions throughout the Empire.

Until his death in 340 A.D., Nicholas continued
his travels and good works, some of which were
subsequently recognized as miracles. While his
miraculous acts included restoring the lives of a
dead sailor and later three boys who had been
horribly murdered, Nicholas was best known for
his generosity, as the following story relates:

The Gift of St. Nicholas

ADAPTED FROM BUTLER'S
"LIVES OF THE SAINTS"

*A*s a young man in Asia Minor, Nicholas was quite wealthy, but unlike other well-to-do swains, he sought to put his money to good use. One day, Nicholas learned of a poor nobleman who had three lovely daughters. While each had a favorite suitor, none could hope to be married without a dowry. Indeed, their father had so little money that he feared they would starve or that he might have to sell them off into slavery.

One night, the poor nobleman stood by the window of his humble dwelling looking sadly up at the moon, ruing his daughters' fates, when a round object sailed past him and landed on the floor. It was a pouch, and when the man undid the ties, he found several pieces of gold. Overjoyed, the grateful father called to his eldest daughter and told her of their good fortune. In the morning, she found the young man whom she wished to marry, and a match was arranged with the dowry of gold coins.

*T*he nobleman was happy for his eldest, but as he stood by the window the following night, his heart ached for his second daughter. Surely such a miracle could not be repeated. But just then, another pouch of gold coins flew in the window. The man raced outside to see who his benefactor was, but to no avail. He returned inside and told his middle child the good news. Again, in the morning, the lovely maiden hurried to the suitor who wished her hand in marriage, and arrangements were made for their union.

The nobleman was relieved at this turn of events, but he was curious. That night, a little before the time he had come to the window the previous evenings, he sneaked into the alley outside his home and waited. Sure enough, a dark figure came up to the window and was about to hurl another bag of coins, when the nobleman grabbed his cloak and revealed Nicholas, known as one of the richest men in the city. The grateful father fell to his knees and thanked the young man, but could not resist asking why he insisted on hiding his identity.

Nicholas answered simply, "This is how I prefer it. You must promise me that you will not reveal my identity." The older man promised, and the young man left a third bag of coins in the nobleman's hand and disappeared into the dark. The father brought the coins into the house and told the joyous news to his youngest, who like her older sisters had no trouble finding a young man to whom she would be betrothed.

And though the secret was kept for a few days, eventually the daughters prevailed upon their father to reveal the identity of their patron. He told them, on the condition that they would keep the secret, but like all secrets too wonderful to hold, the news of Nicholas's generosity soon spread far and wide. And that is why each December children eagerly await the arrival of St. Nicholas, the generous man who secretly leaves gifts while they sleep.

*R*ussians have always had an affinity for St. Nicholas, but *D'yed Moroz*, or Grandfather Frost, became the Russian Santa Claus during Soviet rule. Since the early 19th century, St. Nick and later Grandfather Frost have been depicted wearing the familiar red suit, fringed with white fur. Like the American Santa, Frost does not arrive with a family's gifts until all the children are asleep. In the countryside, however, this tradition did not catch on until relatively recently. Russian farmers, however, had another "frost" tradition. Hoping to prevent the cold from frosting their crops in the coming year, they laid out sweets and other food each Christmas to appease Grandfather Frost and his chilling winds.

British children write letters to Father Christmas with their lists of presents, but instead of mailing them to the North Pole, they throw them into the fireplace. The blaze escapes up the chimney, and Father Christmas, from his heavenly perch, is able to read the smoke signals. On Christmas Eve, the English Claus, like his American counterpart, is inclined to slip down one's chimney. In fact, it is said that on one Christmas he dropped some gold coins while shimmying down a particularly narrow passage. Had it not been for a stocking hung out to dry by the fire, the coins would have fallen down the ash grate. English children (and their American brothers and sisters) therefore hang out stockings, hoping that they will "catch" anything extra Father Christmas drops.

The Czech Santa Claus is *Svaty Mikalas*. He is believed to slip down to earth from heaven along with his companions—an angel and a whip-carrying devil (the latter presumably to punish little boys and girls who have been bad). In earlier days the Dutch Santa Claus, *Sinterklaas,* who sails from Spain on December 6, the Feast Day of St. Nicholas, had a similarly fearsome aspect, carrying a birch rod for the naughty. Today he is generally more agreeable. Dutch children hedge their bets anyway, filling their shoes with hay and sugar for *Sinterklaas'*s horse on the night of December 5. In the morning, they are rewarded with nuts and candy, as well as other presents.

Danish children wait for *Julemanden,* who arrives with a sack of gifts on his back, in a sleigh drawn by reindeer. Children leave bowls of milk or rice pudding for him and his elves, called *Julenisser,* who are said to live in attics. In Norway, Santa is not Santa at all, but *Julebukk,* a goat-like gnome. And in Sweden, Christmas's bearer of good tidings is known as *Jultomar,* a species of gnome said to live under the floor of the house or barn.

*T*oday, the Three Wise Men or Kings, who traveled from the East wearing splendid robes and bearing exotic gifts for the Christ Child, are as well-known as they are loved. St. Matthew mentioned their visit, and through the centuries legends grew about these mysterious travelers.

Some historians have identified the Magi (a name given to a high caste among Medes and Persians) as Melchior (a ruler of Nubia and Arabia), Balthazar (of Ethiopia), and Kaspar (of Tarsus). Journeying from Babylon, they had heard the prophecy that a bright star would herald the arrival of the Messiah. With an Eastern star guiding them, they traveled to Jerusalem—their provisions, according to legend, never needing to be replenished. After questioning people there, and arousing Herod's suspicions about the birth of a new leader, the Wise Men saw the star, which had diminished, burning brightly again. They

followed this beacon to Bethlehem, where they offered the Christ Child their gifts of gold, frankincense, and myrrh.

The Feast of the Epiphany marks the visit of the Three Wise Kings to Bethlehem. *La Befana*, "the woman of the Epiphany," is a central figure not only in the Italian lore surrounding the Wise Men, but in Italy's holiday gift-giving traditions. According to legend, the Magi, during their journey, asked an old woman for food and shelter, which she refused. A few hours later, however, she saw the error of her parsimony and rushed to find the travelers, but she was too late. They were gone. Today described as a fairy, a crone, or a witch, *La Befana* still wanders the earth, searching for the Magi and the Christ Child each Epiphany. And each January 6, Italian children await her visit, sometimes with trepidation, for *La Befana* brings gifts for children who are good, but punishment for the bad.

In Spain, gifts are exchanged on the Epiphany, and the Wise Men are the focus of the celebration. In particular, Balthazar is a favorite, and children leave straw, carrots, and barley out on the night of January 5th for his weary donkey.

*C*hrist's humble birth in the manger beside an inn has had several cultural incarnations.

The first Nativity scene originated in Italy. St. Francis of Assisi, no doubt enamored of the animals that populated the original manger, asked an artisan, Giovannie Vellita of Greccio, to create a manger scene or *presèpio*. St. Francis held a wonderful Mass in front of Vellita's work, inspiring others to recreate the *presèpio* with similar figures called *pastori*.

In France, nearly every home has a *crèche*, or Nativity scene, often decorated with beautiful clay figures called *santons* or "little saints." Since the 17th century, craftsmen in the South of France

have been renowned for these figurines—colorful depictions of the Holy Family, shepherds, Magi, and local dignitaries.

American families of Central and South American descent share Europeans' fascination with the Nativity; *nacimientos*, or *presepios*, are centerpieces of their celebrations. Many are elaborate, filling an entire room with figures made to scale. There are often magnificent landscapes, with shepherds and their flocks looking down on Bethlehem from lush green hills. In addition to the traditional characters, particularly lavish displays boast water mills, grottoes, and even electric sailboats by the sea. Nativity scenes also appear in churches, homes, and public places throughout the United States.

The Nativity has been the inspiration not only for *crèches* or *presepios*, but also for Christmas plays. Among the most elaborate of these spectacles is *Los Pastores*, or "The Shepherds." When performed in its entirety, this venerable miracle play can last as long as five hours. In most cases, however, shorter sections of *Los Pastores* are performed, particularly *Las Posadas*, or "The Lodgings." These performances are not formally staged, but take place with the help of several families or an entire community. Together, in the streets and in their homes, the performers re-enact Joseph and Mary's search for a place to stay in Bethlehem.

As the Holy Couple needed nine days to reach Bethlehem from Nazareth, the first performance of *Las Posadas* usually comes nine days before

Christmas. It is then repeated each evening until Christmas Eve. Some families play the part of pilgrims, while others are innkeepers. The pilgrims travel to each of the innkeepers' homes, where they are denied shelter. Finally, they reach the home where an altar and a *nacimiento* have been erected. The group then says a traditional prayer, food and drink are served, and blindfolded children may take turns swinging a stick at the *piñata*, a papier mâché or earthenware vessel that breaks apart to reveal a bounty of treats.

O TANNENBAUM, O TANNENBAUM

*C*hristmas trees are the floral focal point of the contemporary holiday, and the Christmas tree tradition has a long and storied past, probably stemming from a 10th-century legend. This tale describes how on the night Christ was born, all the trees, though covered in ice and snow, flowered and bore fruit. A later German folk tale tells the story of a shivering child who came to a woodcutter's home in the middle of winter. The child was warmly welcomed and given a bed to sleep in. That morning, a choir of angels sang in the sky, and the woodcutter and his family discovered that they had cared for the Christ Child the night before. The Child, upon leaving his warm-hearted hosts, picked a twig from a fir tree and planted it. He said that the tree would

never fail to bear fruit at Christmas and that the woodcutter's family would always live in abundance—which they did.

The origin of the domestic Christmas tree is often ascribed to the 16th-century reformer Martin Luther. One Christmas, it is said, he took a walk outdoors and was entranced by the stars and nature's beauty. When he came home, he told his children to set up a tree and attach candles to symbolize the beautiful heavens that produced Jesus.

In the ensuing centuries, the German Christmas tree grew more elaborate. Candy canes, glass balls, cookies, sweets, and oranges were used to decorate the tree, and a star was generally placed on the top—traditions that remain in one form or another to this day.

While 18th-century German immigrants to America brought many of their customs with them, Christmas was officially suppressed in some parts of the colonies, particularly New England.

Indeed, we must travel back to England, and wait until the middle of the 19th century, and the reign of Queen Victoria and Prince Albert, to trace the origin of the Christmas tree's popularity in the United States.

*I*n 1841, at Christmas time, these English monarchs decorated a table-top fir tree—to the delight of children and adults. The custom quickly spread, and these trees grew in size until they had to be taken off the table. Soon they became the symbol of a family-oriented Christmas.

Victorian decorations were edible—shiny red apples, strings of popcorn, walnuts painted gold, barley sugar, and other confections. In fact, early trees were often called "sugartrees" because of the sweet quality of the decorations. When the tree was dismantled on January 5th, the eve of the Epiphany, the sweets would be raffled off to a family's eager children.

The English passion for Christmas trees soon found its way back across the Atlantic, though some Protestant sects continued to denounce the tradition for its pagan roots. It was not until the turn of the century that a second wave of German immigration firmly established the tree in the American Christmas celebration. At that time, many Americans imported artificial trees from Germany. These trees, made of feathers dyed green and attached to wire limbs, were generally under three feet tall. World War I, however, turned Americans' Christmas affections to more natural domestic products—Douglas fir, white pine, red pine, Scotch pine, spruce, and balsam fir. Today, electric lights, wooden toys, and beautiful ornaments are hallmarks of contemporary American Christmas trees.

The Lumberjack's Miracle

ADAPTED FROM
"THE MIRACLE OF THE FIR TREE,"
BY JEAN VARIOT,
TRANSLATED BY LEON KING

It was a cold and windy Christmas Eve in a small logging village in far Northern Vermont, and a small boy, clothed in a light cloth jacket, wandered from house to house, dragging a ragged fir tree, which he tried to sell. He made his arduous rounds because both his parents were ill, and his sister was still an infant. The little boy was his family's only wage earner.

"Would you like to buy a small Christmas tree," he asked plaintively at each door. The answer, however, was always the same. "We would have loved to buy your tree, but you are too late. It's Christmas Eve, and we already have one."

*A*fter working his way through this dispiriting routine several times, the boy found himself at the edge of town at the house of Frank Mosher, a lumberjack. He knocked at the door.

"Who could it be at this hour, and on Christmas Eve?" the little boy heard Frank say to his wife and children. He did not sound happy, and the small boy shuddered as much from his fear of the big man's temper as from the cold.

When the door opened, a rush of warm air overwhelmed the small boy. There was a huge tree, complete with decorations and presents, a roaring fire, and a Christmas feast ready for the eating.

"What do you want, little boy," the lumberjack bellowed, "and what are you doing with that pitiful tree?"

The boy trembled, but managed to blurt
out, "I wanted to sell this tree for Christmas,
but you already have such a beautiful one."

"Never mind," said Frank, "I'll buy yours."
He fetched a coin and gave it to the boy.
"Well come in, young man," he said, "and
join us." The boy could not believe his ears,
but when he felt the heat of the fire up close
and tasted the first juicy piece of turkey, he
realized that this was no dream. When he
had finished eating, the boy almost skipped
home. Seeing the coin, his family rejoiced
at his good luck.

The next day, after all the Christmas festivities
had concluded, Frank's wife, Meredith, began
to clean up. She gathered all the wrapping
paper and garbage and the boy's straggly
tree, and left them all out by the street. The
Mosher children, fidgety from being inside
all morning, went outside to play before
going to church. When they saw their mother
throwing out the tree, they decided that they
would pretend they were lumberjacks like
their father. They would plant the tree and
chop it down.

It was then time for church, so the children dragged the tree along with them and, before they went in, planted the little fir in the snow next to the chapel. They would chop it down later.

Inside the church, the music of the organ rose up, and Frank looked over his happy, if slightly unruly brood. He bowed his head reverently and prayed for God to bless his family. During the service, Frank's eyes wandered upon a small *crèche*, prettily decorated in one corner of the church. He thought to himself of the Christ's humble beginnings as a poor young child.

When the service was over, Frank and his family stood up to leave. As they waited patiently to file out, they heard a great commotion outside the church. When they got outside, they could not believe their eyes. Towering above the steeple, a tremendous fir tree grew proudly into the blue sky, and all around the tree's thick heavy branches, doves, as white as the steeple itself, proclaimed the Glory of God.

*A*dvent Wreath

The Christmas wreath, beloved today for its scent
and color, was originally fashioned as a symbol of
Christ's crown of thorns. Wreaths are formed from
a variety of natural materials—pine, cedar and
yew, hawthorn, holly, and laurel—and are made
in all shapes and sizes.

Advent wreaths—evergreen loops with four
candles affixed—are a festive tradition brought
to the United States from Germany. Some
wreaths feature lavender candles, symbolizing
the penitence one should feel in preparing for
the celebration of Christ's birth. Others use red
candles in keeping with the holiday color scheme.
The first candle is lit on the first Sunday after

November 26, the second and third on the following two Sundays, and the last on Christmas Eve itself. Often the family will join around the wreath for each lighting, read a short prayer or scripture, and perhaps sing a hymn or carol. The weekly practice is a lovely and powerful stimulant to the Christmas spirit, a reminder that the holy day is fast approaching.

Poinsettia

Native to Central America, the plant is named for Dr. Joel Roberts Poinsett, who served as U.S. Ambassador to Mexico in the 1820s. When he returned home to South Carolina, he brought the broad-leafed plant with him, and it spread widely. In Mexico, the plant is called "the flower of the Holy Night," and a Mexican legend explains this appellation.

The story goes that a young shepherd boy traveled with the Three Wise Men to offer gifts to the Christ Child. Dismayed because he did not have a gift for the baby, he prayed fervently while the group paused in their journey. When the boy arose, the poinsettia miraculously grew where he had knelt. His prayers answered, the boy took a stalk of the plant with its vermilion blooms, and when he arrived in Bethlehem he laid his gift at the feet of the Christ Child.

Cherry Blossom

The cherry tree has a special place in Christmas celebrations in the Czech Republic and Poland. There, people break off branches of a cherry tree at the beginning of Advent and place them indoors in pots of water. The warm air causes the twigs to bloom and, by Christmas, cherry blossoms fill the house. These blossoms are considered good luck charms. An unmarried woman who tends a twig carefully will find a husband in the next year, it is said, if the bloom is produced on Christmas Eve.

In the English legend, "The Cherry Tree Carol," a cherry tree, responding miraculously to the unborn Christ Child in Mary's womb, bends down to let Mary eat its fruit. After she tastes the cherries, an angel appears and announces that she will bear the Savior.

Today, cherry blossoms, like the other flowering plants mentioned above, are little miracles in and of themselves. Like the miraculous birth of Christ, they remind us that even in darkest, coldest winter, spring's warmth and light are never far behind.

Mistletoe

Mistletoe, known now for its romantic connotations, was for many centuries a symbol of healing and divine love. Just before the Reformation, clergy at England's Cathedral of York began bringing a large bundle of mistletoe into the cathedral each Christmas. This healing plant served as a symbol of Christ, the Divine Healer of all people and nations.

In the years that followed, the people of England gradually introduced mistletoe into their homes, where the more familiar traditions surrounding the plant developed. Hanging mistletoe in a doorway or from the ceiling became a sign of good will and harmony to all visitors—a throwback to mistletoe's ancient role as a "plant of peace."

In old England, kissing under the mistletoe was considered a sincere pledge of love and marriage. In fact, unless one kissed under the plant at Christmas, one's chances of exchanging vows during the following year were considered slim.

This ritual began when a man kissed a woman under the mistletoe. He then took berries off the mistletoe, and they were saved as tokens of love. When all the berries were plucked, all the kissing was done. On the Twelfth and final night of Christmas, the mistletoe was burned. Otherwise, supposedly, the couples who had kissed beneath it would never marry.

In America, mistletoe remains a symbol of warmth and friendship, happiness and good luck. And while a kiss under the mistletoe may not be interpreted as a proposal of marriage, it still warms the heart and adds to the excitement and good cheer around the holidays.

Merry Christmas